Grade 3 Piano

Improve your scales!

Paul Harris

FABER *ff* MUSIC

Introduction

Scales and arpeggios *are* important. And if taught and learned imaginatively, they can be fun!

Improve Your Scales! is designed to help you approach scale learning methodically and thoughtfully. Its intention is to turn learning scales into a pleasant, positive and relevant experience by gradually building up the skills to play them through cumulative and enjoyable activities.

What *Improve Your Scales!* is about

The idea of *Improve Your Scales!* is to present you with lots of engaging activities that lead up to playing the scale (and arpeggio). Actually playing the scale is the last thing that you do! These activities build up an understanding (of the fingering, technical issues, the sound, particular features, sense of key and connections with the pieces that you play) to help make the learning of scales really relevant.

At the top of each scale is a keyboard showing the notes of that particular scale (the minor keys have two keyboards for the melodic minor pattern). This is for you to fill in with whatever you find most useful. Here are some suggestions:
- highlight or colour in the notes of the scale – so you can see the pattern of black and white notes.
- fill in the note names.
- add the fingering you will use for both hands.

Here are two really important **Golden Rules**:

No 1 Before practising your scales make sure that you:
- Drink some water (this helps get the brain working!)
- Relax (especially shoulders, arms, wrists and fingers)
- Check your posture.

No 2 Always practise the scale and arpeggio of the pieces you are learning.

Acknowledgements
Firstly a big thank you to Diana Jackson who, through her considerable and distinguished teaching experience, has furnished many valuable thoughts and ideas.

Thanks also to Claire Dunham whose terrific eye for detail has been invaluable. Also to my own teacher Graeme Humphrey who helped so much in preparing the first edition, and Ann Priestley for many useful comments.

Finally, huge thanks to Lesley Rutherford, my wonderful editor at Faber Music, who always goes well beyond the call of duty.

Fingering made easy!

There are actually only a few fingering patterns used for scales. Once you have these clearly in your mind you'll realise that fingering scales is really easy to master!

Every basic scale (major or minor) has eight notes – but we only have five fingers. So we have to devise simple repetitive patterns that will allow us to play the scales comfortably and fluently. Once you understand the pattern you've virtually learnt to play the scale!

Most of the scales in grade 3 still use the basic C major finger pattern. There are just four new patterns you will have to learn:

B♭ major for comfort and ease, thumbs are rarely used on black notes in scales, so a new pattern needs to be learnt.
RH: 2 **1**23 **1**234 **1**23 **1**234
LH: **3**21 **4**321 **3**21 **4**321 **2**

E♭ major
RH: 2 **1**234 **1**23 **1**234 **1**23
LH: **3**21 **4**321 **3**21 **4**321 **2** (as B♭ major)

B major and minor
RH: uses the basic C major pattern
LH: **4**321 **4**321 **3**21 **4**321

Think about why these patterns have been devised and why they work well. It will make learning them more straightforward.

Arpeggios

There are three finger patterns for the arpeggios at this grade; one fits all the arpeggios that begin on a white note:

RH: **1**23 **1**235
LH: uses 3 or 4 for the second note depending on the interval

The right-hand fingering for the two black note arpeggios is the same:
RH: 2 **1**24 **1**24
But for comfort, the best left-hand fingering is:
B♭ LH: **3**21 **3**21 **2**
E♭ LH: **2**1 **4**21 **4**2

Aim to play arpeggios evenly – don't accent every three notes.

The complete scale and arpeggio are given on pages 25 and 29.

A major

Fill in the scale:
(See page 2 for details of how to do this.)

Write the key signature of A major (treble
and bass clefs):

Finger fitness

> **TOP TIP** Try playing your scales and exercises
> with different dynamics, including crescendo
> and diminuendo.

1

2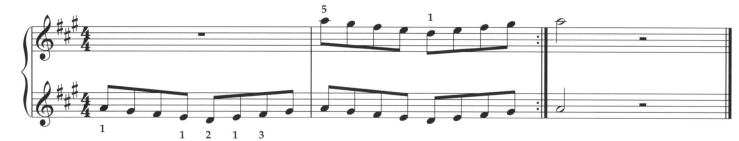

3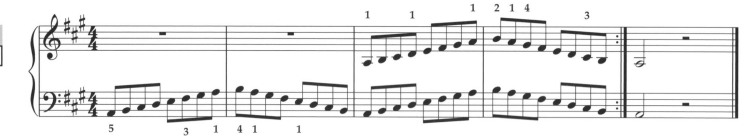

Practise each 2-bar phrase of exercise 4 until it is really under control, then play it complete.

4

Always practise each bar of exercises 5 and 6 separately; then practise the whole exercise,
repeating it until you are confident and fluent.

5

6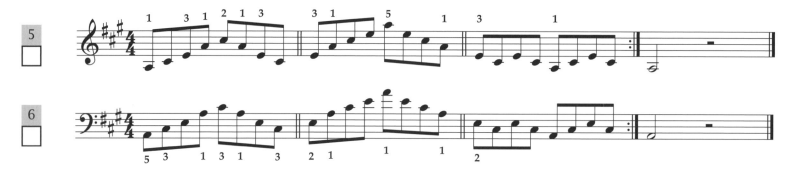

1

Key piece   Anteater antics

2

Have a go Using both hands (you may like to
continue the left-hand drone), or just the right-hand
line, compose or improvise an answering phrase or a
short piece beginning with these notes:

3

Sight-reading

1 In which key is this piece?

2 Can you spot any repeated patterns?

3 What will you count? Tap the rhythm of each line separately, then both lines together.

4 How will you bring character to your performance?

5 Try to hear the music in your head before you begin.

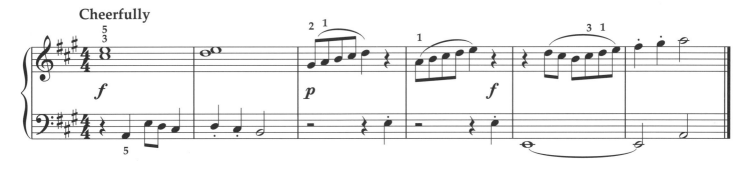

See also *Improve your sight-reading* Piano Grade 3, Stage 3: A major.

4

You are now ready to **say** the notes, **hear** the scale or broken chord in your head (playing
the keynote first), **think** about the fingering and then finally **play** the scale and arpeggio
with confidence!

The complete scale and arpeggio are given on pages 25 and 29.

E major

Fill in the scale:

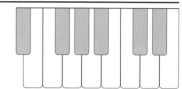

Write the key signature of E major (treble and bass clefs):

> **TOP TIP** E major has a distinctive pattern of two pairs of black keys.

Finger fitness

1

Key piece   Ecossaise

2

Have a go Using both hands, or just the right-hand line, compose or improvise an answering phrase or a short piece beginning with these notes:

3

Sight-reading

1 In which key is this piece?

2 Can you find the scale and arpeggio patterns?

3 What will you count? Tap the rhythm of each line separately, then both lines together.

4 Try to hear the music in your head before you begin.

4

You are now ready to **say** the notes, **hear** the scale or broken chord in your head (playing the keynote first), **think** about the fingering and then finally **play** the scale and arpeggio with confidence!

B major

Fill in the scale:

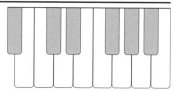

Write the key signature of B major (treble
and bass clefs):

Finger fitness

> **TOP TIP** Although there are many sharps in this
> key signature, it is one of the most comfortable
> scales to play. It uses all the black notes, plus the
> lower of the 2 white keys each time.

1

Key piece   Ballet

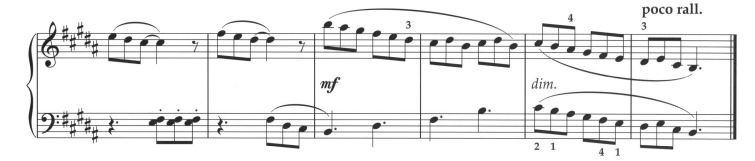

2

Have a go Using both hands, or just the right-hand line, compose or improvise an answering phrase or a short piece beginning with these notes:

3

Sight-reading

1 In which key is this piece?

2 Which notes are not sharpened?

3 What will you count? Tap the rhythm of each line separately, then both lines together.

4 Where will you have to change hand position?

5 Try to hear the music in your head before you begin.

4

You are now ready to **say** the notes, **hear** the scale or broken chord in your head (playing the keynote first), **think** about the fingering and then finally **play** the scale and arpeggio with confidence!

The complete scale and arpeggio are given on pages 25 and 29.

B♭ major

Fill in the scale:

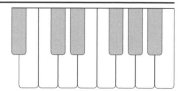

Write the key signature of B♭ major (treble and bass clefs):

> **TOP TIP** This is your first scale to start on a black note. Thumbs are rarely used on black keys in scales, so you'll need to learn some new patterns (see page 3).

Finger fitness

1

Key piece   Brass band

2

Have a go Using both hands, or just the right-hand line, compose or improvise an answering phrase or a short piece beginning with these notes:

3

Sight-reading

1 In which key is this piece?

2 Think about the fingering of the chords, left hand bars 1-4.

3 What will you count? Tap the rhythm of each line separately, then both lines together.

4 How will you convey the character of the piece?

5 Try to hear the music in your head before you begin.

See also *Improve Your Sight-reading* Grade 3, Stage 5: B♭ major.

4

You are now ready to **say** the notes, **hear** the scale or broken chord in your head (playing the keynote first), **think** about the fingering and then finally **play** the scale and arpeggio with confidence!

The complete scale and arpeggio are given on pages 26 and 29.

E♭ major

Fill in the scale:

Write the key signature of E♭ major (treble and bass clefs):

TOP TIP This scale also begins on a black note, with a new finger pattern to avoid playing any black keys with your thumb.

Finger fitness

1

Key piece   Escalator

2

Have a go Using both hands, or just the right-hand line, compose or improvise an answering phrase or a short piece beginning with these notes:

3

Sight-reading

1 In which key is this piece?

2 Can you spot the scale patterns? Are there any repeated rhythmic patterns?

3 What will you count? Tap the rhythm of each line separately, then both lines together.

4 How will you convey the character of the piece?

5 Try to hear the music in your head before you begin.

See also *Improve Your Sight-reading* Grade 3, Stage 6: E♭ major.

4

You are now ready to **say** the notes, **hear** the scale or broken chord in your head (playing the keynote first), **think** about the fingering and then finally **play** the scale and arpeggio with confidence!

B minor

Fill in the scale:

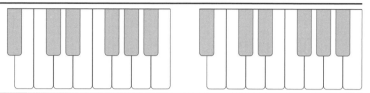

Write the key signature of B minor
(treble and bass clefs):

The relative major of B minor is: _____

> **TOP TIP** In this scale, the right hand uses the
> conventional fingering and the left hand has
> a new pattern. When both hands play, thumbs
> always come together, except on the top note.

Finger fitness

Harmonic exercises

Arpeggio exercises

Melodic exercises

7

8

9

1

Key piece   **Barcarolle**   Using B harmonic minor

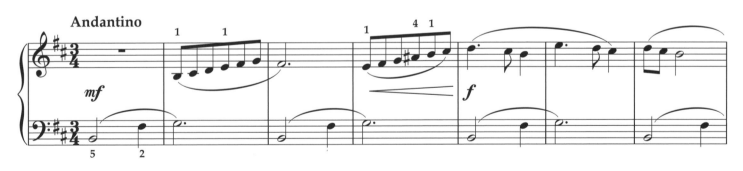

2

Key piece   Ballad   Using B melodic minor

3

Have a go   Using both hands, or just the right-hand line, compose or improvise an answering phrase or a short piece beginning with these notes:

4

Sight-reading

1 In which key is this piece?

2 Can you spot the scale and arpeggio patterns? Which form of the scale is used?

3 What will you count? Tap the rhythm of each line separately, then both lines together.

4 Are there any repeated rhythmic patterns?

5 Try to hear the music in your head before you begin.

See also *Improve Your Sight-reading* Grade 3, Stage 4: B minor.

5

You are now ready to **say** the notes, **hear** the scale or broken chord in your head (playing the keynote first), **think** about the fingering and then finally **play** the scale and arpeggio with confidence!

Paul Harris's Exam Workout!

IMPROVE YOUR SIGHT-READING!

The ability to sight-read fluently is an important part of musical training, whether intending to play professionally, or simply for enjoyment. By becoming a good sight-reader, the player will be able to learn pieces more quickly, pianists will accompany more easily and all musicians will play duets and chamber music with confidence and assurance. Also, in grade examinations, a good performance in the sight-reading test will result in useful extra marks!

Improve your sight-reading! is a series of workbooks designed to help incorporate sight-reading regularly into practice and lessons, and to help prepare for the sight-reading test in grade examinations. It offers a progressive series of enjoyable and stimulating stages which, with careful work, should result in considerable improvement from week to week.

Step by step, the player is encouraged to build up a complete picture of each piece. Rhythmic exercises help develop and maintain a steady beat, whilst melodic exercises assist in the recognition of melodic shapes at a glance. The study of a prepared piece with associated questions for the student to answer helps consolidate acquired skills and, finally, the real, unprepared sight-reading test itself. Mark-boxes for each stage help keep a check on progress.

Such practical and methodical material is guaranteed to take the horror out of sight-reading!

0-571-53300-0	Piano Pre-Grade 1	NEW EDITION
0-571-53301-9	Piano Grade 1	NEW EDITION
0-571-53302-7	Piano Grade 2	NEW EDITION
0-571-53303-5	Piano Grade 3	NEW EDITION
0-571-53304-3	Piano Grade 4	NEW EDITION
0-571-53305-1	Piano Grade 5	NEW EDITION
0-571-53306-X	Piano Grade 6	NEW EDITION
0-571-53307-8	Piano Grade 7	NEW EDITION
0-571-53308-6	Piano Grade 8	NEW EDITION
0-571-51385-9	Violin Grade 1	
0-571-51386-7	Violin Grade 2	
0-571-51387-5	Violin Grade 3	
0-571-51388-3	Violin Grade 4	
0-571-51389-1	Violin Grade 5	
0-571-51735-8	Violin Grade 6	
0-571-51736-6	Violin Grade 7–8	
0-571-51075-2	Viola Grades 1–5	

0-571-51873-7	Cello Grades 1–3
0-571-51874-5	Cello Grades 4–5
0-571-51149-X	Double Bass Grades 1–5
0-571-51373-5	Descant Recorder Grades 1–3
0-571-51466-9	Flute Grades 1–3
0-571-51467-7	Flute Grades 4–5
0-571-51789-7	Flute Grade 6
0-571-51790-0	Flute Grades 7–8
0-571-51464-2	Clarinet Grades 1–3
0-571-51465-0	Clarinet Grades 4–5
0-571-51787-0	Clarinet Grade 6
0-571-51788-9	Clarinet Grades 7–8
0-571-51635-1	Saxophone Grades 1–3
0-571-51636-X	Saxophone Grades 4–5
0-571-51633-5	Oboe Grades 1–3
0-571-57021-6	Oboe Grades 4–5
0-571-51148-1	Bassoon Grades 1–5
0-571-51076-0	Horn Grades 1–5
0-571-50989-4	Trumpet Grades 1–5
0-571-51152-X	Trumpet Grades 5–8
0-571-56860-2	Trombone Grades 1–5

IMPROVE YOUR AURAL!

The very thought of aural, especially in examinations, strikes fear into the heart of many young pianists and instrumentalists. But aural should not be an occasional optional extra – it's something to be developing all the time, because having a good ear will help improve musicianship more than any other single musical skill.

Improve your aural! is designed to take the fear out of aural. Through fun listening activities, boxes to fill in and practice exercises, these workbooks and CDs focus on all the elements of the ABRSM aural tests. Because all aspects of musical training are of course connected, the student will also be singing, clapping, playing their instrument, writing music down, improvising and composing – as well as developing that vital ability to do well at the aural test in your grade exams!

0-571-53438-4	Grade 1 (with CD)	NEW EDITION
0-571-53439-2	Grade 2 (with CD)	NEW EDITION
0-571-53544-5	Grade 3 (with CD)	NEW EDITION
0-571-53545-3	Grade 4 (with CD)	NEW EDITION
0-571-53546-1	Grade 5 (with CD)	NEW EDITION
0-571-53440-6	Grade 6 (with CD)	NEW EDITION
0-571-53441-4	Grades 7–8 (with CD)	NEW EDITION

IMPROVE YOUR PRACTICE!

Improve your practice! is the essential companion for pianists, encapsulating Paul Harris's failsafe approach to learning.

With boxes for filling in, make-your-own playing cards, a handy practice diary and, when needed, an exam countdown, these books help to explore the pieces and to understand their character. The books will enable the student to develop ways of getting the most out of their practice sessions – whatever their length.

Most importantly, the wider musical skills such as aural, theory, sight-reading, improvisation and composition develop alongside, resulting in a more intelligent and all-round musician. Practice makes perfect!

0-571-52844-9	Piano Beginners
0-571-52261-0	Piano Grade 1
0-571-52262-9	Piano Grade 2
0-571-52263-7	Piano Grade 3
0-571-52264-5	Piano Grade 4
0-571-52265-3	Piano Grade 5
0-571-52271-8	Instrumental Grade 1
0-571-52272-6	Instrumental Grade 2
0-571-52273-4	Instrumental Grade 3
0-571-52274-2	Instrumental Grade 4
0-571-52275-0	Instrumental Grade 5

IMPROVE YOUR TEACHING!

Energising and inspirational, **Improve your teaching!** and **Teaching Beginners** are 'must have' handbooks for all instrumental and singing teachers. Packed full of comprehensive advice and practical strategies, they offer creative yet accessible solutions to the challenges faced in music education.

These insightful volumes are distilled from years of personal experience and research. In his approachable style, Paul Harris outlines his innovative strategy of 'simultaneous learning' as well as offering advice on lesson preparation, aural and memory work, effective practice and more.

0-571-52534-2	Improve your teaching!
0-571-53175-X	Improve your teaching! Teaching beginners
0-571-53319-1	Group Music Teaching in Practice (with ECD)

IMPROVE YOUR SCALES!

Paul Harris's **Improve your scales!** is the only way to learn scales.

The purpose of the workbooks is to incorporate regular scale playing into lessons and daily practice, and to help pupils prepare for grade examinations. Each volume contains all the scales, arpeggios and ranges required for the relevant Associated Board exam, along with complementary practical material. 'Know your notes!' makes sure the actual notes are known!; 'finger fitness' exercises strengthen fingers and cover technically tricky areas and the scales, arpeggios and broken chord study pieces place the material in a more musical context. Simple improvisations and even an opportunity to 'have a go' at composing a short tune encourage thought 'in the key'.

This unique approach encourages the student to understand and play comfortably within in a key, thus helping them pick up those valuable extra marks in exams, as well as promoting a solid basis for the learning of repertoire and for sight-reading.

0-571-53411-2	Piano Grade 1	NEW EDITION
0-571-53412-0	Piano Grade 2	NEW EDITION
0-571-53413-9	Piano Grade 3	NEW EDITION
0-571-53414-7	Piano Grade 4	NEW EDITION
0-571-53415-5	Piano Grade 5	NEW EDITION
0-571-51664-5	Violin Grade 3	
0-571-51665-3	Violin Grade 4	
0-571-51666-1	Violin Grade 5	
0-571-51663-7	Violin Grades 1–2	
0-571-52024-3	Flute Grades 1–3	
0-571-52025-1	Flute Grades 4–5	
0-571-51475-8	Clarinet Grades 1–3	
0-571-51476-6	Clarinet Grades 4–5	

Faber Music Limited
Burnt Mill, Elizabeth Way, Harlow, Essex CM20 2HX. Tel: +44 (0)1279 828982 Fax: +44 (0)1279 828983
www.fabermusic.com

G minor

Fill in the scale:

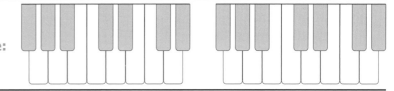

Write the key signature of G minor (treble and bass clefs):

The relative major of G minor is: _____

TOP TIP Try practising your scales and exercises with different rhythms, such as:
♪. ♪ ♪. ♪ and ♪ ♪. ♪ ♪.

Finger fitness

1

Harmonic exercises

2

3

4

Arpeggio exercises

5

6

Melodic exercises

7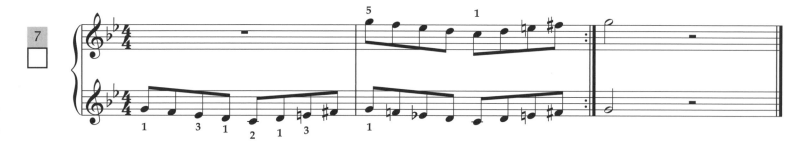

8

9

1 # Key piece   **Gossamer**   Using G harmonic minor

2

Key piece   **Graceful ghost**   Using G melodic minor

3

Have a go Using both hands, or just the right-hand line, compose or improvise an answering phrase or a short piece beginning with these notes:

4

Sight-reading

1 In which key is this piece?

2 Can you spot the scale and arpeggio patterns? What pattern can you see in the left hand, bars 1 and 2?

3 What will you count? Tap the rhythm of each line separately, then both lines together.

4 Are there any repeated rhythmic patterns?

5 Try to hear the music in your head before you begin.

See also *Improve Your Sight-reading* Grade 3, Stage 5: G minor.

5

You are now ready to **say** the notes, **hear** the scale or broken chord in your head (playing the keynote first), **think** about the fingering and then finally **play** the scale and arpeggio with confidence!

C minor

Fill in the scale:

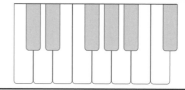 

Write the key signature of C minor (treble and bass clefs):

The relative major of C minor is: _____

TOP TIP Try practising your scales and exercises with different articulations, eg: ♩♩♩♩ and ♩♩♩♩

Finger fitness

1

Harmonic exercises

2

3

4

Arpeggio exercises

5

6

Melodic exercises

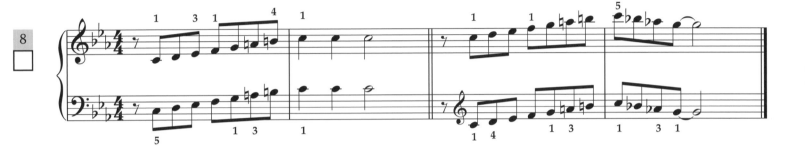

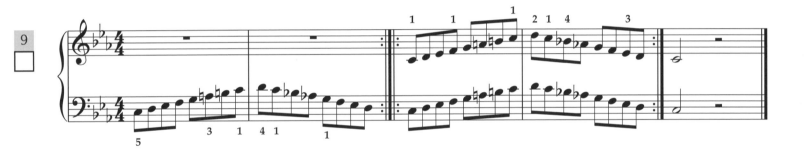

Key piece   **Crystals**   Using C harmonic minor

2

Key piece   **Clouds**   Using C melodic minor

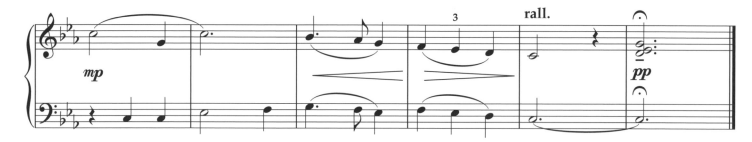

3

Have a go Using both hands, or just the right-hand line, compose or improvise an answering phrase or a short piece beginning with these notes:

4

Sight-reading

1 In which key is this piece?

2 Can you spot the scale and arpeggio patterns? What pattern can you see in the right hand, bars 5 and 6?

3 What will you count? Tap the rhythm of each line separately, then both lines together.

4 What interesting feature can you see in bar 1 and also in bar 3?

5 Try to hear the music in your head before you begin.

5

You are now ready to **say** the notes, **hear** the scale or broken chord in your head (playing the keynote first), **think** about the fingering and then finally **play** the scale and arpeggio with confidence!

Contrary motion scale studies

Your left hand is probably used to ascending and then descending, so work at the left hand carefully first. Try playing the scale with your eyes closed! When confident, add the right hand.

1

Acrobats Contrary motion scale study in A major

2

Angry alligator Contrary motion scale study in A harmonic minor

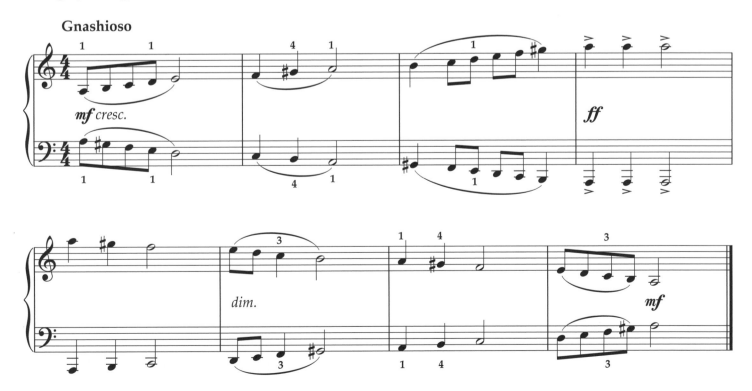

Chromatic scale study

The most common fingering for chromatic scales uses 1, 2 and 3
(3 always plays a black note). Chromatic passages are usually showy,
so should be played smoothly and fast, to impress! Remember:

- To make a 'C' shape with thumb and 3rd finger and keep the rest of
the hand steady when you play.

- There are two places where there are two white notes together – the
2nd finger is used to fill in the extra white note each time.

- To listen carefully for a smooth and unaccented musical line.

Crazy chromatics

Complete Grade 3 scales

For Grade 3 exams, the minimum scale tempo is ♩ = 80, and ♩ = 69 for arpeggios. Try practising with a metronome, increasing the speed one notch at a time.

Exam requirements of the Associated Board:

- *Scales* major and minor (melodic or harmonic at candidate's choice):
  In similar motion with hands together one octave apart, and with each hand separately, in the following keys:
  A, E, B, B♭, E♭ majors (two octaves)
  B, G, C minors (two octaves)

- *Contrary motion scales* with both hands beginning and ending on the key-note (unison)
  in the keys: A major and A harmonic minor (two octaves)

- *Chromatic scales* each hand separately: A♭ and C (two octaves)

E♭ major

B minor harmonic

B minor melodic

G minor harmonic

G minor melodic

☐ **C minor harmonic**

☐ **C minor melodic**

☐ **A major contrary motion**

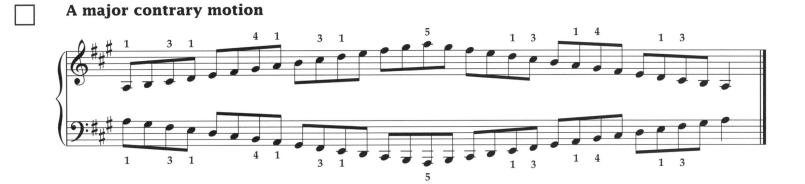

☐ **A harmonic minor contrary motion**

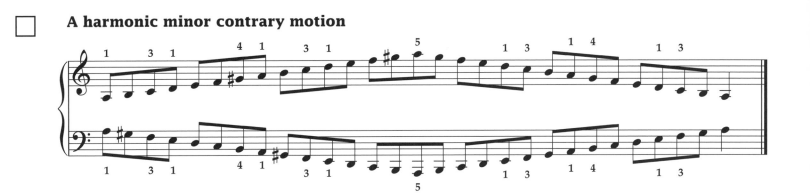

Chromatic scale beginning on A♭

Chromatic scale beginning on C

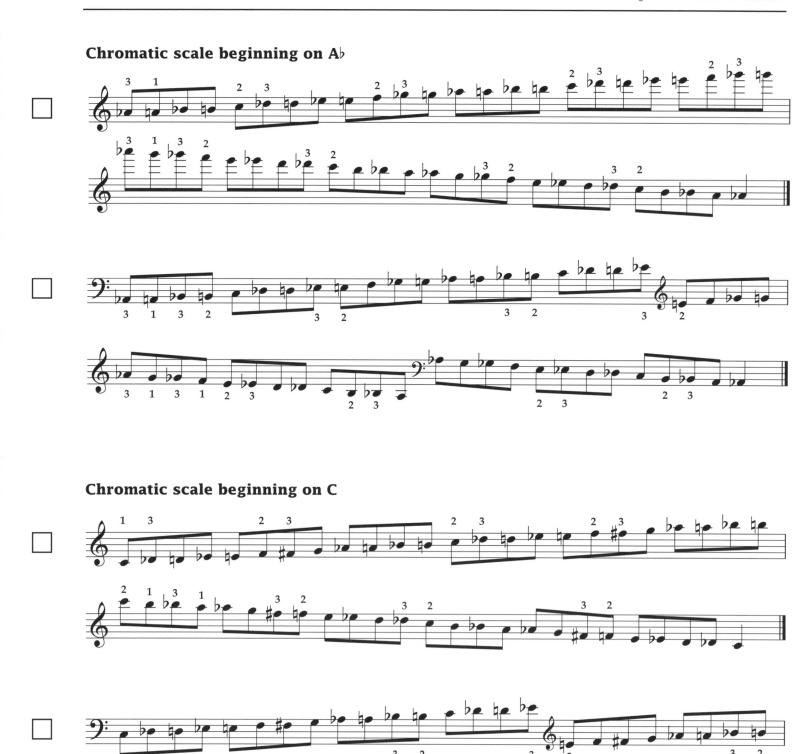

Exam requirements of the Associated Board:

- *Arpeggios of E, B, B♭ and E♭ majors*, and *C and B minors* in root position only with each hand separately (two octaves)

- *Arpeggios of A major and G minor* hands together (two octaves)

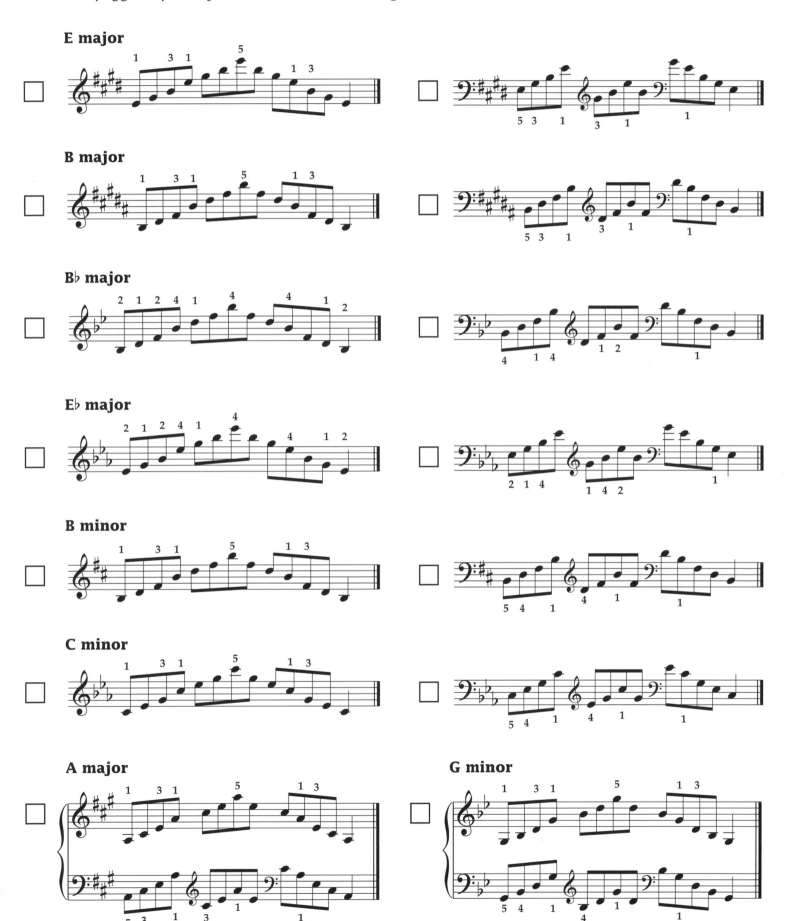

E major

B major

B♭ major

E♭ major

B minor

C minor

A major

G minor

Why are scales important?

There are many reasons and it's important that pupils know these! Scales will hugely improve all aspects of your finger technique, facility and control.

- Arpeggios will improve your ability to move around the piano with ease.
- Knowing your scales and arpeggios will speed up the learning of new pieces because so much material is usually based on scale and arpeggio patterns.
- Knowing your scales and arpeggios will improve your sight reading both in dealing with technical issues and reading melodic patterns.
- Knowing your scales and arpeggios will develop your sense of key.
- Playing scales and arpeggios well and with confidence will earn good marks in exams.

Scales and exams

So that's why scales are an important part of exams! They really do help to develop your playing. In an exam, the examiner will be listening out for:
- A prompt response
- Evenness of pulse and rhythm
- Control and evenness of tone
- No unnecessary accents
- The smooth passage of the thumb
- A sense of key
- Fluency and dexterity
- A musical shape for each example

Think about each of these during practice sessions. Tick them off in your mind.

Practice chart

Practise your scales in different ways – with different rhythms and dynamics and thinking of different colours and flavours!

Scale/Arpeggio	Comments	Tick a box each time you practise											
A major													
Scale (hands separately and together)													
Arpeggio (hands together)													
E major													
Scale (hands separately and together)													
Arpeggio (hands separately)													
B major													
Scale (hands separately and together)													
Arpeggio (hands separately)													
B♭ major													
Scale (hands separately and together)													
Arpeggio (hands separately)													
E♭ major													
Scale (hands separately and together)													
Arpeggio (hands separately)													
B minor													
Scale (hands separately and together)													
Arpeggio (hands separately)													
G minor													
Scale (hands separately and together)													
Arpeggio (hands together)													
C minor													
Scale (hands separately and together)													
Arpeggio (hands separately)													
Contrary motion in A major													
Contrary motion in A harmonic minor													
Chromatic starting on C													
Chromatic starting on A♭													

© 2010 Faber Music Ltd
First published in 1995 by Faber Music Ltd
Bloomsbury House 74–77 Great Russell Street London WC1B 3DA
Music processed by Donald Thomson
Cover and text designed by Susan Clarke
Printed in England by Caligraving Ltd

ISBN10: 0-571-53413-9
EAN13: 978-0-571-53413-5

To buy Faber Music publications or to find out about the full range of titles
available please contact your local music retailer or Faber Music sales enquiries:
Faber Music Ltd, Burnt Mill, Elizabeth Way, Harlow CM20 2HX
Tel: +44 (0) 1279 82 89 82   Fax: +44 (0) 1279 82 89 83
sales@fabermusic.com   fabermusic.com